Tolstoy

in Search of Truth and Meaning

Wisdom
from his Letters, Novels, Essays
and Conversations

Leo Tolstoy

Edited by Bob Blaisdell

ixia
PRESS

Garden City, New York

This Ixia Press edition, first published in 2024, is a new selection reprinted from standard texts. A new introduction has been specially prepared for this edition.

ISBN-13: 978-0-486-85238-6
ISBN-10: 0-486-85238-5

Publisher: Betina Cochran
Acquisitions Editor: Fiona Hallowell
Managing Editorial Supervisor: Susan Rattiner
Production Editor: Gregory Koutrouby
Cover Designer: Mark Voss
Creative Manager and Interior Designer: Marie Zaczkiewicz
Production: Pam Weston, Tammi McKenna, Ayse Yilmaz

IXIA PRESS
An imprint of Dover Publications

Manufactured in China
85238501   2024
www.doverpublications.com/ixiapress

Contents

Introduction

I much dislike, or rather am often uncomfortable, when people too well-disposed towards me take me seriously, seeking and demanding a complete correspondence between my words and my deeds. "How is it you say this, and do that?"

Yes, I am not a Saint, and have never given myself out for one. I am a man, often carried away; and sometimes, or rather always, saying not quite what I think and feel—not that I do not wish to say it, but that I am unable, and often exaggerate, or simply blunder. That is so in words. In deeds the case is yet worse. I am quite a weak man, of vicious habits, who wishes to serve the God of Truth, but constantly goes astray.

—*Leo Tolstoy*[1]

The Russian aristocrat Leo Nikolaevich Tolstoy was born in 1828 on the estate where he spent most of his life. He was, as a thinker, like a carpenter who hammered his planks hard and true. And yet he was also like the architect who then pried off those very boards from the floors and walls to start the construction over again. In this collection we will see his continual efforts and the patterns of his thoughts about life's primary meanings and goals. "I am eighty years old," he wrote to a correspondent in 1908, "and I am still searching for truth."[2]

---

[1] Letter to D. A. Khilkov, February 1, 1892, translated by Aylmer Maude.
[2] Letter to an Old Believer, December 16, 1908, translated by Aylmer Maude.

The quotations I have selected are not the impersonalized nuggets of wisdom that he manufactured from his readings and from his own philosophical and religious writings in the last years of his world-famous life, and then arranged in three editions. These quotations are instead, as Tolstoy himself remarks about the posthumously published private journal of Henri Amiel, "the inner labor of his soul," the continual revelation of Tolstoy's strivings toward truths that guided his efforts to be good and useful. They are, I believe, "live" representations of a colossal literary genius's lifelong struggle to steady and direct himself and to understand life's purpose.

The quotations come from his earliest surviving diary (begun when he was eighteen); his fiction (published from the time he was twenty-three until his death—and after); religious writings; political tracts; conversations with his acquaintances and visitors; and letters to his family, friends, and, as in the case of his inspirational note to Mohandas Gandhi, worldwide correspondents.

In Tolstoy's fiction, when the characters pursue their personal truths and purposes, the author almost always shows us the range and depth of their daily lives, the details and circumstances of which often correspond to those in his own very particular life. In the context in which the characters (and he) live, the fiction demonstrates the challenges of sustaining any state of philosophical or spiritual balance. In the conclusion of *Anna Karenina*, the Tolstoy-like Levin, who has momentarily found peace of mind after an extended period of existential despair, reflects:

"This new feeling has not changed me, has not made me happy and enlightened all of a sudden, as I had dreamed, just like the feeling for my child. There was no surprise in this either. Faith—or not faith—I don't know what it is—but this feeling has come just as imperceptibly through suffering, and has taken firm root in my soul.

"I shall go on in the same way, losing my temper with Ivan the coachman, falling into angry discussions, expressing my opinions tactlessly; there will be still the same wall between the holy of holies of my soul and other people, even my wife; I shall still go on scolding her for my own terror, and being remorseful for it; I shall still be as unable to understand with my reason why I pray, and I shall still go on praying; but my life now, my whole life apart from anything that can happen to me, every minute of it is no more meaningless, as it was before, but it has the positive meaning of goodness, which I have the power to put into it."[3]

Enlightenment, like marriage, requires continual effort and renewal.

I read Tolstoy in much the same way as he instructs us to read the New Testament: "To understand any book one must choose out the parts that are quite clear, dividing them from what is obscure or confused. And from what is clear we must form our idea of the drift and spirit of the whole work. Then, on the basis of what we have understood, we may proceed to make out what is confused or not quite intelligible. [. . .] Very likely in selecting what is, from what is not, fully comprehensible, people will not all mark the same

---

[3] *Anna Karenina* (1877–78), translated by Constance Garnett.

passages. What is comprehensible to me may seem obscure to another. But all will certainly agree in what is most important, and there are things which will be found quite intelligible to everyone."[4] For this project I have read and reread thousands of pages and have even discovered works I had somehow always overlooked; the passages that I marked and gathered were where Tolstoy's words seemed to resonate through his life and, I admit, often through my own.

Tolstoy was an inexhaustible and brilliant reader and synthesizer of his reading. He spent various periods in the final phase of his life pruning and refining the wisdom that he had found and derived from world literature, religion, and philosophy, and presented these works not only in *A Calendar of Wisdom* but also in *The Path of Life* (*Put' Zhizni*) and in his most ambitious anthology, *A Cycle of Reading* (*Na Kazhdyy Den'*); he even quoted and paraphrased examples from his own wisdom. (For example, from the entry for December 23: "Scholarship rarely mixes with wisdom. A scholar knows a lot of things, but the largest part of it is unnecessary and doubtful. A wise person, however, knows few things, but everything that he knows is necessary to him and to the people, and that which he knows is certain.") I, on the other hand, prefer his unrefined, seemingly spontaneous revelations, where he is actively pursuing—and once in a while discovering and celebrating or regretting—the deepest truths of his or his characters' lives.

In my experience, there has never been so vital and vitalizing a writer: powerful, clear, very occasionally amusing, almost always deadly serious. I hope with these selections to reveal Tolstoy not as a sage detached from life, but fully immersed in and challenged by life: an intense

---

[4] "How to Read the Gospels and What Is Essential in Them" (1896), translated by Aylmer Maude.

person, writer, father, husband—*and* sage. He is almost never boring, but sometimes even to his loved ones and admirers (I count myself a wholehearted admirer), he can be exasperating.

When in religious works and articles he arrives at particular profundities (e.g., "There is no other love than that which lays down its life for a friend. Love is only really love when it is a sacrifice of self"[5]), I confess that I hear my own skepticism. I also imagine his wife Sofia Tolstaya's objections, because, in his boiled-down thoughts, Tolstoy has boiled off his complicated and complicating life experiences—that is, he has disregarded one of the most notable qualities of his fiction. Such refined thoughts are *only* thoughts, detached from the meat and bones of his whole self. For me, Tolstoy is whole only when he is seeking, only when he is weighed down by the gravity (or spurred by the energy) of his own body and he faces the dilemmas of everyday life: "Nekhlyudov always made some rules for himself which he meant to follow forever after, wrote his diary, and began afresh a life which he hoped never to change again. 'Turning over a new leaf,' he called it to himself in English. But each time the temptations of the world entrapped him, and without noticing it he fell again, often lower than before."[6]

I should mention those of his everyday conflicts that won't make much of an appearance in these pages. For one, I have ignored his shame-ridden renunciations of sex, these from a man whose wife gave birth thirteen times. His thoughts on sexual life and on women's roles in private and public life vary, but, except in his fiction, are rarely enlightened, and I won't pass them along. He has a primary

---

[5] *On Life* (1887), translated by Aylmer Maude.
[6] *Resurrection* (1899), translated by Louise Maude.

forum for them, anyway, in the novella *The Kreutzer Sonata* and its passionate (I won't say hysterical) "Afterword." His friend Anton Chekhov, who was a doctor as well as a great writer, remarked on "the audacity with which Tolstoy treats topics about which he knows nothing and which out of obstinacy he does not wish to understand. For example, his opinions on syphilis, foundling homes, women's revulsion for sexual intercourse, and so on are not only debatable, they expose him as an ignorant man who has never at any point in his long life taken the trouble to read two or three books written by specialists. Nevertheless, these faults are as easily dispersed as feathers in the wind; the worth of the work [i.e., *Resurrection*] is such that they simply pass unnoticed. And, if you do notice them, the only result is that you find yourself annoyed it has not escaped the fate of all human works, all of which are imperfect and tainted."[7]

Yes, nobody's perfect, not even our heroes![8] "When people consider me as one who cannot make a mistake," Tolstoy reflected to a correspondent in 1892, "every error seems like a lie or a piece of hypocrisy. But if I am understood to be a weak man, the discord between my words and acts appears as a sign of weakness, but not as a lie or a hypocrisy. And then I appear to be what I am: a sorry but sincere man, now and always wishing with his whole soul to be quite good; to be, that is, a worthy servant of God."[9]

But by my lights and by those of his great English biographer, translator, and friend, Aylmer Maude, there

---

[7] *Anton Chekhov's Life and Thought: Selected Letters and Commentary*, selected by Simon Karlinsky, translated by Michael Henry Heim and Karlinsky. Berkeley: University of California Press, 1973. 155–7.

[8] In his early seventies, Tolstoy remarked to a young admirer, the author Maxim Gorky: "Heroes — that's a lie and invention; there are simply people, people, and nothing else." Maxim Gorky, *Reminiscences of Tolstoy*, translated by S. S. Kotelianksy and Leonard Woolf.

[9] Letter to D. A. Khilkov, February 1, 1892, translated by Aylmer Maude.

has never been a greater, more important writer. "While piecing together the scattered and sometime seemingly contradictory facts of his life," Maude reflects at the conclusion of his comprehensive Tolstoy biography, most of which was written while Tolstoy was alive, "I have realized more vividly than ever before how great my own debt to him is, and how inadequately this record conveys his spiritual value. That side of my subject takes me out of my depth, and the message necessarily suffers from the deficiencies of the messenger."[10]

Though I sometimes pretend I know the details and outlines of Tolstoy's life as well as or better than my own, in my search for *his* search for the meaning of life, I have been surprised by the consistency of his personality. This has led me to decide to arrange the quotations more or less chronologically in connection to his life experiences. That is, his 1852 novella *Childhood*, about the experiences of a young boy who is similar to but not identical to himself, I have placed in the time when Tolstoy was a child. (Similarly I have so arranged the quotations from the sequels to that work, his novellas *Boyhood* and *Youth*.) I have placed the quotations from his philosophical works in line with when he was writing them rather than when he published them, as occasionally censorship (due to his criticism of the Russian Orthodox Church and the Russian government) delayed or barred their publication. Quotations from his most upsetting and most personal of autobiographical writings,

---

[10] In one of Aylmer Maude's final letters to Tolstoy, who had been cooperating in Maude's two-volume work about his life, the biographer writes: "I owe you so much, that I never differ from any of your opinions without regret, or without remembering that perhaps, after all, I am mistaken; but I feel that it would violate the very essence of what I learnt from you, if I subordinated the truth as I see it, to any authority—even to your own." Aylmer Maude, *The Life of Tolstoy, Later Years* (1910).

Confession, I have primarily placed in the "Crisis" years that he refers to, when he was most depressed, rather than in the year of its publication (1882). His posthumously published works, some of which were incomplete, I have placed in their time of writing, or in the years that reflect his own similar experiences (e.g., *Father Sergius* and "Fedor Kuzmich").

I hope, thereby, that not only will Tolstoy's thoughts and reflections stir up your own contemplation and memories (as they have mine), but that a major biographical theme will carry us, as along a river, through his long life. I have started each section with biographical notes on the given period that follows. There are excellent biographies of Tolstoy, among them those by Aylmer Maude, Ernest J. Simmons, Pavel Birukov, and Tolstoy's daughter Alexandra Tolstaya, as well as two from this century by Rosamund Bartlett and Andrei Zorin. The best revelation of the complete man and literary genius remains, however, in his fiction, from *Childhood* and *The Cossacks* to *War and Peace*, *Anna Karenina*, and *Hadji Murad*.

I thank Professor Michael A. Denner, editor of *Tolstoy Studies Journal*, for his suggestions and encouragement.

For the English translations of Tolstoy's work I have relied on public domain versions and my own renderings. (For a complete list of the translators and the passages each has translated, see the note in the Selected Bibliography, p. 97.) I have used American spellings (e.g., *labor* rather than *labour*) and only very occasionally updated or revised an obscure word or phrase in my predecessors' excellent translations. I use bracketed ellipses [. . .] to indicate a deletion; the other ellipses are from the sources.

—*Bob Blaisdell*

Part 1

Thoughts on Childhood, Boyhood, Youth

Leo Nikolaevich Tolstoy, the fourth of four sons, followed by a sister, was born in 1828 at the family estate about 120 miles south of Moscow, Yasnaya Polyana. His mother died in 1830, and his father died in 1837. As a boy he was primarily raised by his aunts at Yasnaya Polyana and in Moscow and Kazan. At the age of sixteen, he began attending the university in Kazan, which he left, without earning a degree, when he was eighteen.

Was I not alive when I learned to look, to listen, to understand, and to speak, when I slept, took the breast, kissed it, and laughed and gladdened my mother? I lived, and lived blissfully! Did I not then acquire all that by which I now live, and acquire it to such an extent and so quickly, that in all the rest of my life I have not acquired a hundredth part of the amount? From a five-year-old child to my present self there is only one step. From a new-born infant to a five-year-old child there is an awesome distance. From the germ to the infant is an unfathomable distance. But from non-existence to the germ the distance is not only unfathomable, but inconceivable.

—"First Recollections"

In a mysterious way, incomprehensible to the human mind, the impressions of early childhood are preserved in one's memory, and not only are they preserved, but they grow in some unfathomed depth of the soul, like seed thrown on good ground, and after many years all of a sudden thrust their vernal shoots into God's world.

—"Reminiscences"

[. . .] all those who surrounded my infancy, from my father to the coachman, appear to me as exceptionally good people. Probably my pure loving feeling, like a bright ray, disclosed to me in people their best qualities (such always exist); when all these people seemed to me exceptionally good I was much nearer the truth than when I saw only their defects.

—"Reminiscences"

[. . .] it was Nikolenka [Tolstoy's eldest brother, Nikolay] who, when I [was] five years old, Mitenka [brother Dmitry] six, Seryozha [brother Sergey] seven, announced to us that he possessed a secret by means of which, when it should be disclosed, all men would become happy: there would be no diseases, no troubles, no one would be angry with anyone, all would love each other, all would become "Ant brothers." He probably meant "Moravian brothers," about whom he had heard and had been reading [. . .]. The ant brotherhood was revealed to us, but the chief secret as to the way for all men to cease suffering any misfortune, to leave off quarrelling and being angry, and to become continuously happy, this secret, as he told us, was written by him on a green stick, which stick he had buried by the road on the edge of a certain ravine, at which spot, since my corpse must be buried somewhere, I have asked to be buried in memory of Nikolenka. [. . .] As then I believed that there existed a little green stick whereon was written that which could destroy all the evil in men and give them great welfare, so do I now also believe that such truth exists, and that it will be revealed to men and will give them all that it promises.

—"Reminiscences"

Happy, happy, irrecoverable time of childhood! How not love, how not cherish its memories? Those memories refresh and lift my soul and serve me as the source of the sweetest pleasures. [. . .] Will it ever be possible to return to that freshness, carefreeness, the need for love, the strength of faith that you possess in childhood? What period could be better than when the two supreme virtues—innocent joy and an infinite need for love—were the only inducements in life?

—*Childhood*

He was nine years old; he was a child; but he knew his own soul, it was precious to him, he guarded it as the eyelid guards the eye, and without the key of love he let no one into his soul. His teachers complained that he would not learn, while his soul was brimming over with thirst for knowledge. And he learned from Kapitonich [the porter], from his nurse, from Nadinka [a young girl], from Vassily Lukitch [the tutor], but not from his teachers. The spring his father and his teachers reckoned upon to turn their mill-wheels had long dried up at the source, but its waters did their work in another channel.

—*Anna Karenina*

Has it ever happened to you, my reader, at a certain point in life, you suddenly notice that your view of things has absolutely changed, as if all the objects that you had seen until then suddenly turned to you another yet unknown side? Such a moral transformation came to me for the first time during our journey, from which I count the beginning of my adolescence. For the first time the clear thought came into my head that we were not the only ones; i.e., our family, we're living in a world whose interests do not revolve around us, and that there exists another life, of people who have nothing in common with us, don't care about us, and even do not have an awareness of our existence. No doubt I knew all this before; but I knew it not in the way I now knew it; I wasn't conscious of it; I didn't feel it.

—*Boyhood*

Who would believe what the favorite and most constant subjects of my ponderings at this time of my adolescence were—they were so out of keeping with my age and situation. [. . .] Once, suddenly remembering that death awaited me every hour, every minute, I was puzzled, not understanding how people hadn't already understood this, and I decided that a person could not be happy except by indulging themselves in the present and not thinking of the future—and I, for about three days, under the influence of this thought, tossed aside my lessons, and only occupied myself by lying in bed pleasure-reading some novel and eating honey-cakes, which I had bought with my last bit of money. [. . .]

I imagined that, besides me, no one and nothing existed in the whole world, that objective things were not objective things but images, making themselves visible only when I turned my attention on them, and that as soon as I stopped thinking about them, the images immediately vanished. In a word, I was going along with [the philosopher Frederich Wilhelm] Schelling in the conviction that objects did not exist, but only my relationship to them. There were moments that I, under the influence of this *idée fixe*, reached the stage of extreme behavior that sometimes I would quickly glance to the opposite side, hoping to catch off-guard the nothingness there, just where I wasn't.

—Boyhood

... being under the influence of [my friend] Nekhlyudov, I unconsciously followed his direction, the essence of which was an enthusiastic worship of the ideal of virtue and the conviction that life's purpose is constantly perfecting oneself. At that time, correcting humankind, eliminating all the vices and all personal unhappiness seemed doable—it seemed very easy and simple to correct myself and partake of all the virtues and be happy.

— *Boyhood*

The religious doctrine taught me from childhood disappeared in me as in others, but with this difference, that as from the age of fifteen I began to read philosophical works, my rejection of the doctrine became a conscious one at a very early age. From the time I was sixteen I ceased to say my prayers and ceased to go to church or to fast of my own volition. I did not believe what had been taught me in childhood but I believed in something. What it was I believed in I could not at all have said. I believed in a God, or rather I did not deny God—but I could not have said what sort of God. Neither did I deny Christ and his teaching, but what his teaching consisted of I again could not have said.

Looking back on that time, I now see clearly that my faith—my only real faith—that which apart from my animal instincts gave impulse to my life—was a belief in perfecting myself. But in what this perfecting consisted and what its object was, I could not have said. I tried to perfect myself mentally—I studied everything I could, anything life threw in my way; I tried to perfect my will, I drew up rules I tried to follow; I perfected myself physically, cultivating my strength and agility by all sorts of exercises, and accustoming myself to endurance and patience by all kinds of privations. And all this I considered to be the pursuit of perfection. The beginning of it all was of course moral perfection, but that was soon replaced by perfection in general: by the desire to be better not in my own eyes or those of God but in the eyes of other people. And very soon this effort again changed into a desire to be stronger than others: to be more famous, more important and richer than others.

—*Confession*

❧

Writing 10 volumes of philosophy is easier than putting one such principle of it into practice.

—Diary, March 17, 1847

❧

I keep finding myself facing the question: "What is the purpose of a person's life?" And no matter where my reflections start, whatever I take as life's source, I keep coming to the same conclusion: The goal of a person's life is making every possible contribution to the all-sided development of all existence.—If I judge by looking at nature, I see that everything in it constantly develops and that each established part of it is made use of unconsciously toward the development of the other parts.

—Diary, April 17, 1847

I know that you will not believe that I have altered; that you will say: *This is already the twentieth time, and still no good comes of you; you are the most frivolous fellow.* No, I have altered in quite a different way from what I did. Then I used to say to myself, "Well, now, I shall change." But now I see that I have changed, and I say, "I have changed."

Above all, I am now fully convinced that one cannot live by abstract speculation and philosophy, but that it is necessary to live positively, i.e., to be a practical man. This is a great step forward and a great change. This has never once happened with me before.

—Letter to his brother Sergey, February 13, 1849

Part 2

On Idealism and the Pursuit of Knowledge

In 1847, Tolstoy came into his inheritance, the
Yasnaya Polyana estate that was among his mother's
family's properties, as well as the serfs belonging to that
estate. He had by then developed a passion—but not
a talent—for gambling. He tried to reform himself
and the serfs, who were indentured servants, but
the serfs were skeptical of his self-sacrificing motives.
Tolstoy himself, despite the immediate blossoming of
his gargantuan literary talent, was in fact not yet
"a practical man." In 1851, he followed his brother
Nikolai to the war in the Caucasus, where he began
serving as a volunteer and wrote a supreme novella,
Childhood (1852). His military experiences in
the Caucasus bore fruit in, among other works, The
Cossacks (1863) and Hadji Murad (posthumous).
Enrolled as an officer in 1854, he served in Sevastopol
in the Crimean War and published grim accounts
of the battles there. He traveled to St. Petersburg, the
Russian capital, in 1855, but became disillusioned
with the literary crowd, which celebrated him. Soon
thereafter, he resigned as a lieutenant from the army
and returned to his estate. He became engaged, broke
off the engagement, and traveled to Europe in 1857.
When he returned again to Yasnaya Polyana, he
started a free school for the local peasant children and
began writing illuminating articles about education.

At the age of eighteen he was free—as only rich young Russians in the 'forties who had lost their parents at an early age could be. Neither physical nor moral fetters of any kind existed for him; he could do as he liked, lacking nothing and bound by nothing. Neither relatives, nor fatherland, nor religion, nor wants, existed for him. He believed in nothing and admitted nothing. But although he believed in nothing he was not a morose young man, nor self-opinionated, but on the contrary continually let himself be carried away. He had come to the conclusion that there is no such thing as love, yet his heart always overflowed in the presence of any young and attractive woman. He had long been aware that honors and position were nonsense, yet involuntarily he felt pleased when at a ball Prince Sergius came up and spoke to him affably. But he yielded to his impulses only in so far as they did not limit his freedom. As soon as he had yielded to any influence and became conscious of its leading on to labor and struggle, he instinctively hastened to free himself from the feeling or activity into which he was being drawn and to regain his freedom. In this way he experimented with society-life, the civil service, farming, music—to which at one time he intended to devote his life—and even with the love of women in which he did not believe. He meditated on the use to which he should devote that power of youth which is granted to man only once in a lifetime: that force which gives a man the power of making himself, or even—as it seemed to him—of making the universe into anything he wishes: should it be to art, to science, to love of woman, or to practical activities?

—*The Cossacks*

"How stupid is all which I have known, and which I have believed in and loved," he said to himself. "Love, self-sacrifice,—these constitute the only true happiness which is independent of accident!" he repeated, smiling, and waving his hands. He applied this thought to life from every side, and he found its confirmation in life, and in the inner voice which told him, "It is this," and he experienced a novel feeling of joyful agitation and transport. "And thus, I must do good in order to be happy," he thought, and all his future was vividly pictured to him, not in the abstract, but in concrete form, in the shape of a landed proprietor.

He saw before him an immense field of action for his whole life, which he would henceforth devote to doing good, and in which he, consequently, would be happy. He would not have to look for a sphere of action: it was there; he had a direct duty,—he had peasants.

What refreshing and grateful labor his imagination evoked: "To act upon this simple, receptive, uncorrupted class of people; to save them from poverty; to give them a sufficiency; to transmit to them the education which I enjoy through good fortune; to reform their vices which are the issue of ignorance and superstition; to develop their morality; to cause them to love goodness.—What a brilliant and happy future! And I, who will be doing it all for my own happiness, shall enjoy their gratitude, and shall see how with every day I come nearer and nearer to the goal which I have set for myself. Enchanting future! How could I have failed to see it before?"

—"A Landed Proprietor"

"How must I live so as to be happy, and why was I formerly not happy?" And he remembered his previous life, and felt disgusted with himself. [. . .] And suddenly a new light seemed revealed to him. "Happiness," said he to himself, "consists in living for others. That is clear. The demand for happiness is innate in man; therefore it is legitimate. If we seek to satisfy it selfishly: by seeking wealth, fame, comforts, or love, circumstances may render the satisfaction of these desires impossible. [. . .] But what desire is there that can always be satisfied in spite of external conditions? What desire? Love, self-sacrifice!" He was so glad and excited at discovering this, as it seemed to him, new truth, that he jumped up and began impatiently seeking for someone for whom he might quickly sacrifice himself: to whom he might do good, and whom he could love. "Yes; I need nothing for myself!" he kept mentally repeating; "Then why not live for others?"

—*The Cossacks*

I find myself greatly changed morally, and this has been the case so very often. However, I believe such is everyone's fate. The longer one lives the more one changes: you who have got experience, tell me, is not this true? I think that the defects and the good qualities—the background of one's character—will always remain the same, but the way of regarding life and happiness must change with age. A year ago I thought I should find happiness in pleasure, in movement; now, on the contrary, rest, both physical and moral, is the state I desire.

—Letter to his aunt, January 12, 1852

Conscience is our best and surest guide, but where are the marks distinguishing this voice from other voices? [. . .] The voice of vanity speaks no less powerfully. For instance—an unrevenged offence. The man whose object is his own happiness is bad; he whose aim is to get the good opinion of others is bad too, he is weak; one whose object is the happiness of others is virtuous; he whose object is God is great.

—Diary, June 29, 1852

And suddenly he was overcome by such a strange feeling of causeless joy and of love for everything, that from an old habit of his childhood he began crossing himself and thanking someone. Suddenly, with extraordinary clearness, he thought: "Here am I, Dmitri Olenin, a being quite distinct from every other being, now lying all alone Heaven only knows where—where a stag used to live—an old stag, a beautiful stag who perhaps had never seen a man, and in a place where no human being has ever sat or thought these thoughts. Here I sit, and around me stand old and young trees, one of them festooned with wild grape vines, and pheasants are fluttering, driving one another about and perhaps scenting their murdered brothers." He felt his pheasants, examined them, and wiped the warm blood off his hand onto his coat. "Perhaps the jackals scent them and with dissatisfied faces go off in another direction: above me, flying in among the leaves which to them seem enormous islands, mosquitoes hang in the air and buzz: one, two, three, four, a hundred, a thousand, a million mosquitoes, and all of them buzz something or other and each one of them is separate from all else and is just such a separate Dmitri Olenin as I am myself." He vividly imagined what the mosquitoes buzzed: "This way, this way, lads! Here's someone we can eat!" They buzzed and stuck to him. And it was clear to him that he was not a Russian nobleman, a member of Moscow society, the friend and relation of so-and-so and so-and-so, but just such a mosquito, or pheasant, or deer, as those that were now living all around him.

—*The Cossacks*

As soon as I am alone and criticize myself I involuntarily return to my former idea—that of perfecting myself; but the chief mistake, the reason I have been unable to go quietly along that road, was that I confused perfecting oneself with perfection. One must first understand oneself and one's defects well and try to remedy them, and not set oneself the task of being perfect, which is not only impossible of attainment from the low point at which I stand, but at the perception of which one loses hope of the possibility of attaining it.

—Diary, July 3, 1854

I have no modesty. That is my great defect. What am I? One of four sons of a retired lieutenant-colonel, left at seven years of age an orphan under the guardianship of women and strangers; having neither a social nor a scholarly education, and becoming my own master at seventeen; with no large means, no social position, and, above all, without principle; a man who has disorganized his own affairs to the last extremity, and has passed the best years of his life without aim or pleasure; and finally who having banished himself to the Caucasus to escape his debts and more especially his bad habits—and having there availed himself of some connection that had existed between his father and the general in command—passed to the army of the Danube at twenty-six, as a Sub-Lieutenant almost without means except his pay (for what means he has he ought to employ to pay what he still owes) without influential friends, ignorant of how to live in society, ignorant of the service, lacking practical capacity, but with immense self-esteem—such is my social position.

—Diary, July 7, 1854

A conversation about divinity and faith suggested to me a great, a stupendous idea, to the realization of which I feel myself capable of devoting my life. This idea is the foundation of a new religion corresponding to the present state of mankind—the religion of Jesus but purified from dogma and mysticism, a practical religion, not promising future bliss, but giving bliss upon earth. I feel that this idea can be realized only by generations consciously looking toward it as a goal. One generation will hand on the idea to the next and, some day, enthusiasm or reason will bring it into being. To act with a deliberate view to the religious union of mankind, this is the leading principle of the idea which I hope will command my enthusiasm.

—Diary, March 5, 1855

My literary goal is fame [and] the good that I am able to do with my writings.

—Diary, September 17, 1855

22

More than once in Nekhlyudov`s life there had been what he called a "cleansing of the soul." By "cleansing of the soul" he meant a state of mind in which, after a long period of sluggish inner life, a total cessation of its activity, he began to clear out all the rubbish that had accumulated in his soul, and was the cause of the cessation of the true life. His soul needed cleansing as a watch does. After such an awakening Nekhlyudov always made some rules for himself which he meant to follow forever after, wrote his diary, and began afresh a life which he hoped never to change again. "Turning over a new leaf," he called it to himself in English. But each time the temptations of the world entrapped him, and without noticing it he fell again, often lower than before.

—*Resurrection*

Nekhlyudov called to mind how he had begun to consider his life in the garden of Kousminsky when deciding what he was going to do, and remembered how confused he had become, how he could not arrive at any decision, how many difficulties each question had presented. He asked himself these questions now, and was surprised how simple it all was. It was simple because he was not thinking now of what would be the results for himself, but only thought of what he ought to do. And, strange to say, what he ought to do for himself he could not decide, but what he ought to do for others he knew indubitably.

—*Resurrection*

"Yes, yes," he thought. "The work that our life accomplishes, the whole of this work, the meaning of it is not, nor can be, intelligible to me. What were my aunts for? Why did Nikolenka Irtenyev die? Why am I living? What was Katusha for? And my madness? Why that war? Why my subsequent lawless life? To understand it, to understand the whole of the Master's will is not in my power. But to do His will, that is written down in my conscience, is in my power; that I know for certain. And when I am fulfilling it, I have sureness and peace."

—Resurrection

"I often lie awake at night from happiness, and all the time I think of our future life together. I have lived through much, and now I think I have found what is needed for happiness. A quiet secluded life in the country, with the possibility of being useful to people to whom it is easy to do good, and who are not accustomed to have it done to them; then work which one hopes may be of some use; then rest, nature, books, music, love for one's neighbor—such is my idea of happiness. And then, on the top of all that, you for a mate, and children, perhaps—what more can the heart of man desire?"

—Family Happiness

[. . .] during my stay in Paris, the sight of an execution revealed to me the instability of my superstitious belief in progress. When I saw the head part from the body, and how they thumped separately into the box, I understood, not with my mind but with my whole being, that no theory of the reasonableness of our present progress could justify this deed; and that though everybody from the creation of the world, on whatever theory, had held it to be necessary, I knew it to be unnecessary and bad; and therefore the arbiter of what is good and evil is not what people say and do, nor is it progress, but it is my heart and I.

—*What I Believe*

"I remember once, when a bear attacked me and pressed me down under him, driving the claws of his enormous paw into my shoulder, I felt no pain, I lay under him and looked into his warm, large mouth, with its wet, white teeth. He breathed above me, and I saw how he turned his head to get into position to bite into both my temples at once; and in his hurry, or from excited appetite, he made a trial snap in the air just above my head, and again opened his mouth —that red, wet, hungry mouth, dripping with saliva. I felt I was about to die, and looked into the depths of that mouth, as one condemned to execution looks into the grave dug for him. I looked, and I remember that I felt no fear or dread. I saw with one eye, beyond the outline of that mouth, a patch of blue sky gleaming between purple clouds roughly piled on one another, and I thought how lovely it was up there. . . . I often remembered that moment afterwards; and now whenever I think of death, I picture that situation to myself, because I have never been nearer to death than then. I recall it, reflect on it, make comparisons, and see that death—real, serious and all-absorbing death—is, thank God, not dreadful. Everything becomes torpid then, and all that causes fear ceases to growl above one's head, and one's soul is easy and at peace. Probably the lamb crunched by a wolf, the bird in the serpent's mouth, travelers attacked in a

25

forest, and men from under whose feet the hangman pushes the stool, feel the same."

—*The Life of Tolstoy*, Maude quotes a conversation of Tolstoy's with Isaak Feinermann (a.k.a. Teneromo) about the real event with the bear in December 1858 and fictionalized in "The Bear Hunt"

We know that our fundamental convictions that the sole educational method is experience, and its sole criterion is freedom, will sound to some like a threadbare banality, for others a muddled abstraction, and for others a daydream and impossibility.

—"On Popular Education"

Part 3

Marriage and Family

In the fall of 1862, Tolstoy fell in love with and married the eighteen-year-old Sofia Behrs, the daughter of a Moscow doctor. They would have six children in the first ten years of their marriage (and Sofia would bear seven more children after that). There was joy, satisfaction, and fulfillment in family life; the Tolstoys were one of those "happy families" that Tolstoy seemed to be thinking of when he wrote the sentence that eventually began Anna Karenina: *"All happy families are alike; each unhappy family is unhappy in its own way." In the first period of marriage, he wrote* War and Peace *(1863–69), and then the* Azbuka *series of language-learning texts and stories (1872–75) that would, over the next hundred years, help teach millions of Russian-speaking children to read. He started composing* Anna Karenina *in 1873.*

Prince Andrey Bolkonsky was lying on the hill of Pratzen, on the spot where he had fallen with the flagstaff in his hands. He was losing blood, and kept moaning a soft, plaintive, childish moan, of which he himself knew nothing. Towards evening he ceased moaning and became perfectly still. He did not know how long his unconsciousness lasted. Suddenly he felt again that he was alive and suffering from a burning, lacerating pain in his head. "Where is it, that lofty sky that I knew not till now and saw today?" was his first thought. "And this agony I did not know either," he thought. "Yes, I knew nothing, nothing. Till now. But where am I?"

He fell to listening, and caught the sound of approaching hoofs and voices speaking French. He opened his eyes. Above him was again the same lofty sky, with clouds higher than ever floating over it, and between them stretches of blue infinity.

—War and Peace

Although five minutes previously Prince Andrey had been able to say a few words to the soldiers who were carrying him, he was silent now, with his eyes fastened directly upon Napoleon. So trivial seemed to him at that moment all the interests that were engrossing Napoleon, so petty seemed to him his hero, with his paltry vanity and glee of victory, in comparison with that lofty, righteous, and kindly sky which he had seen and comprehended, that he could not answer him. And all indeed seemed to him so trifling and useless beside the stern and solemn train of thought aroused in him by weakness from loss of blood, by suffering and the nearness of death. Gazing into Napoleon's eyes, Prince Andrey mused on the nothingness of greatness, on the nothingness of life, of which no one could comprehend the significance, and on the nothingness—still more—of death, the meaning of which could be understood and explained by none of the living.

—War and Peace

The wound in the mother's heart could never be healed. Petya's death had torn away half of her life. When the news of Petya's death reached her, she was a fresh-looking, vigorous woman of fifty; a month later she came out of her room an old woman, half dead and with no more interest in life. But the wound that half killed the countess, that fresh wound, brought [Petya's sister] Natasha back to life.

A spiritual wound that comes from a rending of the spirit is like a physical wound, and after it has healed externally, and the torn edges are scarred over, yet, strange to say, like a deep physical injury, it only heals inwardly by the force of life pushing up from within. So Natasha's wound healed. She believed that her life was over. But suddenly her love for her mother showed her that the essence of her life—love—was still alive within her. Love was awakened, and life waked with it.

—War and Peace

He could not be at peace because after dreaming so long of family life, and feeling himself so ripe for it, he was still not married, and was further than ever from marriage. He was painfully conscious himself, as were all about him, that at his years it is not well for man to be alone. He remembered how before starting for Moscow he had once said to his cowman Nikolay, a simple-hearted peasant, whom he liked talking to: "Well, Nikolay! I mean to get married," and how Nikolay had promptly answered, as of a matter on which there could be no possible doubt: "And high time too, Konstantin Dmitrievich." But marriage had now become further off than ever. [. . .] the recollection of the rejection and the part he had played in the matter tortured him with shame. [. . .] Every week he thought less often of Kitty. He was impatiently looking forward to the news that she was married, or just going to be married, hoping that such news would, like having a tooth out, completely cure him.

—Anna Karenina

He was so far from conceiving of love for woman apart from marriage that he positively pictured to himself first the family, and only secondarily the woman who would give him a family. His ideas of marriage were, consequently, quite unlike those of the great majority of his acquaintances, for whom getting married was one of the numerous facts of social life. For Levin it was the chief affair of life, on which its whole happiness turned.

—Anna Karenina

"You are about to enter into holy matrimony, and God may bless you with offspring. Well, what sort of bringing-up can you give your babes if you do not overcome the temptation of the devil, enticing you to infidelity?" [the priest] said, with gentle reproachfulness. "If you love your child as a good father, you will not desire only wealth, luxury, honor for your infant; you will be anxious for his salvation, his spiritual enlightenment with the light of truth. Eh? What answer will you make him when the innocent babe asks you: 'Papa! Who made all that enchants me in this world—the earth, the waters, the sun, the flowers, the grass?' Can you say to him: 'I don't know'? You cannot but know, since the Lord God in His infinite mercy has revealed it to us. Or your child will ask you: 'What awaits me in the life beyond the tomb?' What will you say to him when you know nothing? How will you answer him? Will you leave him to the allurements of the world and the devil? That's not right," he said, and he stopped, putting his head on one side and looking at Levin with his kindly, gentle eyes.

—*Anna Karenina*

Levin had been married three months. He was happy, but not at all in the way he had expected to be. At every step he found his former dreams disappointed, and new, unexpected surprises of happiness. He was happy; but on entering upon family life he saw at every step that it was utterly different from what he had imagined. At every step he experienced what a man would experience who, after admiring the smooth, happy course of a little boat on a lake, should get himself into that little boat. He saw that it was not all sitting still, floating smoothly; that one had to think too, not for an instant to forget where one was floating; and that there was water under one, and that one must row; and that his unaccustomed hands would be sore; and that it was only to look at it that was easy; but that doing it, though very delightful, was very difficult.

—*Anna Karenina*

As a bachelor, when he had watched other people's married life, seen the petty cares, the squabbles, the jealousy, he had only smiled contemptuously in his heart. In his future married life there could be, he was convinced, nothing of that sort; even the external forms, indeed, he fancied, must be utterly unlike the life of others in everything. And all of a sudden, instead of his life with his wife being made on an individual pattern, it was, on the contrary, entirely made up of the pettiest details, which he had so despised before, but which now, by no will of his own, had gained an extraordinary importance that it was useless to contend against. And Levin saw that the organization of all these details was by no means so easy as he had fancied before.

—*Anna Karenina*

Although Levin believed himself to have the most exact conceptions of domestic life, unconsciously, like all men, he pictured domestic life as the happiest enjoyment of love, with nothing to hinder and no petty cares to distract. He ought, as he conceived the position, to do his work, and to find repose from it in the happiness of love. She ought to be beloved, and nothing more. But, like all men, he forgot that she too would want work. And he was surprised that she, his poetic, exquisite Kitty, could, not merely in the first weeks, but even in the first days of their married life, think, remember, and busy herself about tablecloths, and furniture, about mattresses for visitors, about a tray, about the cook, and the dinner, and so on. While they were still engaged, he had been struck by the definiteness with which she had declined the tour abroad and decided to go into the country, as though she knew of something she wanted, and could still think of something outside her love. This had jarred upon him then, and now her trivial cares and anxieties jarred upon him several times. But he saw that this was essential for her. And, loving her as he did, though he did not understand the reason for them, and jeered at these domestic pursuits, he could not help admiring them.

—Anna Karenina

Ever since, by his beloved brother's deathbed, Levin had first glanced into the questions of life and death in the light of these new convictions, as he called them, which had during the period from his twentieth to his thirty-fourth year imperceptibly replaced his childish and youthful beliefs—he had been stricken with horror, not so much of death, as of life, without any knowledge of whence, and why, and how, and what it was. The physical organization, its decay, the indestructibility of matter, the law of the conservation of energy, evolution, were the words which usurped the place of his old belief. These words and the ideas associated with them were very well for intellectual purposes. But for life they yielded nothing, and Levin felt suddenly like a man who has changed his warm fur-cloak for a muslin garment, and going for the first time into the frost is immediately convinced, not by reason, but by his whole nature, that he is as good as naked, and that he must infallibly perish miserably.

—Anna Karenina

The question was summed up for him thus: "If I do not accept the answers Christianity gives to the problems of my life, what answers do I accept?" And in the whole arsenal of his convictions, so far from finding any satisfactory answers, he was utterly unable to find anything at all like an answer.

He was in the position of a man seeking food in toy shops and tool shops. Instinctively, unconsciously, with every book, with every conversation, with every man he met, he was on the lookout for light on these questions and their solution.

—Anna Karenina

As long as he followed the fixed definition of obscure words such as *spirit, will, freedom, essence*, purposely letting himself go into the snare of words the philosophers set for him, he seemed to comprehend something. But he had only to forget the artificial train of reasoning, and to turn from life itself to what had satisfied him while thinking in accordance with the fixed definitions, and all this artificial edifice fell to pieces at once like a house of cards, and it became clear that the edifice had been built up out of those transposed words, apart from anything in life more important than reason.

—Anna Karenina

". . . Fyodor says that one mustn't live for one's belly, but must live for truth, for God, and at a hint I understand him! And I and millions of men, men who lived ages ago and men living now—peasants, the poor in spirit and the learned, who have thought and written about it, in their obscure words saying the same thing—we are all agreed about this one thing: what we must live for and what is good. I and all men have only one firm, incontestable, clear knowledge, and that knowledge cannot be explained by reason—it is outside it, and has no causes and can have no effects."

"Can I have found the solution of it all? Can my sufferings be over?" thought Levin [. . .].

—Anna Karenina

"What is it makes me glad? What have I discovered? I have discovered nothing. I have only found out what I knew. I understand the force that in the past gave me life, and now too gives me life. I have been set free from falsity, I have found the Master. Of old I used to say that in my body, that in the body of this grass and of this beetle (there, she didn't care for the grass, she's opened her wings and flown away), there was going on a transformation of matter in accordance with physical, chemical, and physiological laws. And in all of us, as well as in the aspens and the clouds and the misty patches, there was a process of evolution. Evolution from what? Into what?—Eternal evolution and struggle. . . . As though there could be any sort of tendency and struggle in the eternal! And I was astonished that in spite of the utmost effort of thought along that road I could not discover the meaning of life, the meaning of my impulses and yearnings. Now I say that I know the meaning of my life: 'To live for God, for my soul.' And this meaning, in spite of its clearness, is mysterious and marvelous. Such, indeed, is the meaning of everything existing."

—Anna Karenina

"This new feeling has not changed me, has not made me happy and enlightened all of a sudden, as I had dreamed, just like the feeling for my child. There was no surprise in this either. Faith—or not faith—I don't know what it is—but this feeling has come just as imperceptibly through suffering, and has taken firm root in my soul.

"I shall go on in the same way, losing my temper with Ivan the coachman, falling into angry discussions, expressing my opinions tactlessly; there will be still the same wall between the holy of holies of my soul and other people, even my wife; I shall still go on scolding her for my own terror, and being remorseful for it; I shall still be as unable to understand with my reason why I pray, and I shall still go on praying; but my life now, my whole life apart from anything that can happen to me, every minute of it is no more meaningless, as it was before, but it has the positive meaning of goodness, which I have the power to put into it."

—*Anna Karenina*

Part 4

Midlife Crisis: Disillusionment and Despair

During the four years of on-again, off-again composing of Anna Karenina, *Tolstoy found himself in the midst of the deepest depression of his life, described in terrifying detail in* Confession *(1882). If there is a dividing line in Tolstoy's life, it is here in the mid- to late-1870s, when he was approaching the age of fifty. Christianity and the truths he derived from all religions and select philosophers became prominent in his daily life. From now to his death at the age of eighty-two, he concentrated regular attention on the meaning of life; this quest sometimes brought him into conflict with the demands or expectations of family life. These conflicts gnawed away at his marriage, though Sofia Tolstaya continued bearing him children through 1888.*

When I go into a school and see this crowd of raggedy, grimy, skinny children with gleaming eyes and so often angelic expressions, alarm finds me, a terror of the kind I might experience seeing people drowning. Oh, Lord—who to rescue? Who first, who rescue later? And that which is drowning is the most valuable quality, namely that soulfulness that is so obviously striking in children. I want education for the people so to save those drowning Pushkins, Ostrogradskis, Filarets, Lomonosovs. They're swarming in every school.

—Letter to Alexandra A. Tolstaya, December 1874

Before occupying myself with my Samara estate, the education of my son, or the writing of a book, I had to know why I was doing it. As long as I did not know why, I could do nothing, and could not live. Amid the thoughts of estate management which greatly occupied me at that time, the question would suddenly occur to me: "Well, you will have 16,000 acres of land in the Samara region and 800 horses, and what next?" . . . And I was quite disconcerted, and did not know what to think. Or, when considering my plans for the education of my children, I would say to myself: What for? Or when considering how the peasants might be prosperous, I suddenly said to myself, "But what business is it of mine?" Or when thinking of the fame my works would bring me, I said to myself, "Very well: you will be more famous than Gogol or Pushkin or Shakespeare or Moliere, or than all the writers in the world—and what will it lead to?" And I could find no reply at all. The questions would not wait, they had to be answered at once, and if I did not answer them, it was impossible to live.

—*Confession*

"Without knowing what I am and why I am here, life's impossible; and that I can't know, and so I can't live," Levin said to himself.

"In infinite time, in infinite matter, in infinite space, is formed a bubble-organism, and that bubble lasts a while and bursts, and that bubble is Me." It was an agonizing error, but it was the sole logical result of ages of human thought in that direction. [. . .]

But it was not merely a falsehood, it was the cruel jeer of some wicked power, some evil, hateful power, to whom one could not submit. He must escape from this power. And the means of escape every man had in his own hands. He had but to cut short this dependence on evil. And there was one means—death.

And Levin, a happy father and husband, in perfect health, was several times so near suicide that he hid the rope that he might not be tempted to hang himself, and was afraid to go out with his gun for fear of shooting himself.

But Levin did not shoot himself, and did not hang himself; he went on living.

—*Anna Karenina*

Once more my soul and my body were tearing themselves apart within me. The same thoughts came again: "I am living, I have lived up till now, I have the right to live; but all around me is death and destruction. Then why live? Why not die? Why not kill myself immediately? No; I could not. I am afraid. Is it better to wait for death to come when it will? No, that is even worse; and I am also afraid of that. Then, I must live. But what for? In order to die?" I could not get out of that circle. I took a book, and began reading. For a moment it made me forget my thoughts. But then the same questions and the same horror came again. I got into bed, lay down, and shut my eyes. That made the horror worse. God had created things as they are. But why? They say, "Don't ask; pray." Well, I did pray [. . .]. But no answer came, as if there were nothing to answer. I was alone, alone with myself and was answering my own questions in place of him who would not answer. "What am I created for?" "To live in a future life," I answered. "Then why this uncertainty and torment? I cannot believe in future life. I did believe when I asked, but not with my whole soul. Now I cannot, I cannot! If Thou didst exist, Thou wouldst reveal it to me, to all men. But Thou dost not exist, and there is nothing true but distress." But I cannot accept that! I rebelled against it; I implored Him to reveal His existence to me.

—"Notes of a Madman"

I had, as it were, lived, lived, and walked, walked, till I had come to a precipice and saw clearly that there was nothing ahead of me but destruction. It was impossible to stop, impossible to go back, and impossible to close my eyes or avoid seeing that there was nothing ahead but suffering and real death—complete annihilation. It had come to this, that I, a healthy, fortunate man, felt I could no longer live: some irresistible power impelled me to rid myself one way or other of life. I cannot say I wished to kill myself. The power which drew me away from life was stronger, fuller, and more widespread than any mere wish. The thought of self-destruction now came to me as naturally as thoughts of how to improve my life had come formerly. And it was so seductive that I had to be wily with myself, lest I should carry it out too hastily: [. . .] And all this befell me at a time when all around me I had what is considered complete good fortune. I was not yet fifty; I had a good wife who loved me and whom I loved; good children, and a large estate which without much effort on my part improved and increased. I was respected by my relations and acquaintances more than at any previous time. I was praised by others, and without much self-deception could consider that my name was famous. And far from being insane or mentally unwell,—on the contrary I enjoyed a strength of mind and body such as I have seldom met with among men of my kind: physically I could keep up with the peasants at mowing, and mentally I could work for eight to ten hours at a stretch without experiencing any ill results from such exertion.

—*Confession*

I lived to my fiftieth year thinking that the life of a person, which proceeds from birth to death, is his whole life and, therefore, the goal of a person is happiness in mortal life, and I tried to obtain this happiness, but the longer I lived the more obvious it became that such happiness is not and cannot exist. The happiness that I was searching for did not come to me; and whatever I achieved, it stopped being happiness. The unhappiness increased all the more, and the inescapability of death became more and more obvious, and I understood that after this meaningless and unhappy life, there was nothing for me to expect besides suffering, illness, old age and extinction. I asked myself: "What's this for?" And I didn't receive an answer and fell into despair.

—"Preface to the Christian Teaching"

To know God and to live is one and the same thing. God is life. Live seeking God, and then you will not live without God. And more than ever before, all within me and around me lit up, and the light did not again abandon me.

—Confession

❀

The more I penetrated the meaning of these books [the Gospels], the more something new appeared to me that was absolutely dissimilar from what the Church teaches but which did answer the question of my life. And finally this answer became completely clear.

And this answer was not only clear, it was doubtless; first off, it fully corresponded with the demands of my reason and heart; secondly, that when I understood it, I saw that the answer was not my exclusive point about the Gospels, as it might seem, and wasn't even exclusive to Christ's revelation, but that this very answer to the question of life is more or less clearly expressed by all humankind's best people, from before and after the Gospels, starting from Moses, Isaiah, Confucius, the ancient Greeks, Buddha, Socrates and all the way to Pascal, Spinoza, Fichte, Feuerbach, and those often unnoticed and unorthodox people who sincerely, without connection to faith-teaching, thought and spoke about the meaning of life. Just so in my consciousness of the Gospel truths, not only wasn't I alone, I was with all the best people of the past and of our time.

—"Preface to the Christian Teaching"

I call revelation that which opens out to us, when reason has reached its utmost limits, the contemplation of what is divine, that is, of truth that is superior to our reason. I call revelation that which gives an answer to the questions, insoluble by reason, which brought me to despair and almost to suicide—the question: What meaning has my life? That answer must be intelligible and must not contradict the laws of reason as would, for instance, the assertion that an infinite number is odd or even. It must not contradict reason, for I shall not believe an answer that does so, and it must be intelligible and not arbitrarily assumed, but inevitable to one's reason as, for instance, a recognition of infinity is to any man who is able to count. The answer must reply to the question: What meaning has my life? A reply that does not answer that question is useless to me. The answer must be such that though its essence may be incomprehensible in itself (as is the essence of God) all the deductions derived from its consequences should correspond to every demand of reason and the meaning it ascribes to my life should solve all my questions as to how to live. The answer must be not merely reasonable and clear but also true, that is, such as I can believe in with my whole soul inevitably, as I believe in the existence of infinity.

—"Introduction to an Examination of the Gospels"

"Well, but you, Leo Nikolaevich: you preach—but what about practice?" That is the most natural of questions; people always put it to me, and always triumphantly shut my mouth with it. "You preach, but how do you live?" And I reply that I do not preach and cannot preach, though I passionately desire to do so. I could only preach by deeds: and my deeds are bad. What I say is not a sermon, but only a refutation of a false understanding of the Christian teaching, and an explanation of its real meaning. Its meaning is not that we should, in its name, rearrange society by violence: its purpose is to find the meaning of our life in this world.

—Letter to M. A. Engelhardt, January 1883

I have become convinced that to convince by logic is not necessary. I have passed through that stage. What I have written and said is sufficient to indicate the path; every seeker will find it for himself, and will find better and fuller arguments more suitable to himself; but the thing is to indicate the path. Now I have become convinced that only one's life can show the path: only the example of one's life. The effect of that example is very slow, very indefinite (in the sense that, I think, one cannot possibly know whom it will influence) and very difficult. But it alone gives a real impulse.

—Letter to V. I. Alekseyev, July 1884

A man lives, and must, therefore, know why he lives. He has established his relation to God; he knows the very truth of truths, and I know the very truth of truths. Our expression may differ; the essence must be the same—we are both of us men. Then why should I—what can induce me to oblige anyone or demand of anyone absolutely to express his truth as I express it? I cannot compel a man to alter his religion either by violence or by cunning or by fraud—false miracles.

His religion is his life. How can I take from him his religion and give him another? It is like taking out his heart and putting another in its place. I can only do that if his religion and mine are words, and are not what gives him life; if it is a wart and not a heart. Such a thing is impossible also, because no man can deceive or compel another to believe what he does not believe; for if a man has adjusted his relation toward God and knows that religion is the relation in which man stands toward God he cannot desire to define another man's relation to God by means of force or fraud.

—"Church and State"

Part 5

Searching for and Finding the Truth

In the 1880s and 1890s, Tolstoy was writing severely about his own moral failings, the government's injustice to the poor and hungry, and the particular ways that Christian churches had corrupted Jesus's primary teachings. His novellas The Death of Ivan Ilych *(1886) and* Master and Man *(1895) pointedly moralize about taking stock of one's life in preparation for death. Tolstoy had found truths that revealed paths forward for himself and, he believed, for humankind. He never relented in trying to hold himself to and declaring to the world Jesus's primary admonition against the use of violence. Tolstoy's bold criticisms of the Russian Orthodox Church for supporting war and government violence caused many of his works to be censored or suppressed. Despite the censorship, his fame and literary power brought his writings in translation to the rest of the world. In 1891, Tolstoy renounced the copyright to all of the work he had produced since 1880.*

Christ does not say, "Offer your cloak and suffer"; but he says, "Resist not him that is evil, and no matter what befalls you do not resist him." These words, "Resist not evil," or "Resist not him that is evil," understood in their direct meaning, were for me truly a key opening everything else, and it became surprising to me that I could so radically have misunderstood the clear and definite words: "It was said, An eye for an eye: and A tooth for a tooth: But I say unto you, Resist not him that is evil, and no matter what he does to you, suffer and surrender, but resist him not." What can be clearer, more intelligible, and more indubitable than that? And I only needed to understand these words simply and directly as they were said and at once Christ's whole teaching, not only in the Sermon on the Mount but in the whole of the Gospels, everything that had been confused, became intelligible; what had been contradictory became harmonious, and, above all, what had appeared superfluous became essential. All merged into one whole, and one thing indubitably confirmed another like the pieces of a broken statue when they are replaced in their true position.

—*What I Believe*

Christ showed me that the fifth snare depriving me of welfare is the distinction we make between our own and other nations. I cannot but believe this; and therefore, if in moments of forgetfulness a feeling of enmity may yet arise in me towards a man of another nationality, I can in quiet moments no longer help acknowledging that feeling to be a bad one. I cannot justify it as I formerly did, by acknowledging the superiority of my people over other nations, or by dwelling on the errors, cruelties, and barbarities of other nations. I cannot but try, at the very first reminder, to be even more friendly to a foreigner than to a compatriot. And beyond knowing that my disunion from other nations is an evil destructive to my welfare, I also know the snare which led me into that evil, and cannot, as I used to do, consciously and calmly promote it. I know that that snare lies in the mistaken conception that my welfare is only bound up with that of my compatriots, and not with that of all people.

—*What I Believe*

I realized that all these unfortunates whom I wished to benefit, besides the hours they spend suffering from hunger and cold, and waiting for a night's lodging, have also time to devote to something else. There is the rest of the twenty-four hours every day, and there is a whole life, about which I had never thought. I here, for the first time, understood that all these people, besides needing food and shelter, must also pass twenty-four hours each day, which they, like the rest of us, have to live. I understood that they must be angry and dull, and must pluck up courage, and mourn and be merry. Strange to say, I now for the first time understood clearly that the business I had undertaken cannot consist merely in feeding and clothing a thousand people as one feeds and drives under shelter a thousand sheep; but that it must consist in doing them good. And when I understood that each of these thousand people was a human being with a past; and with passions, temptations and errors, and thoughts and questions like my own, and was such a man as myself—then the thing I had undertaken suddenly appeared so difficult that I realized my impotence; but it had been started, and I went on with it.

—*What Then Must We Do?*

Don't be angry, darling, that I cannot attribute any importance to those monetary accounts! Such things are not like, for instance, an illness, marriage, birth, death, the acquisition of knowledge, a good or bad action, or the good or bad habits of people near and dear to us; they are things we have devised, which we have arranged this way, and can rearrange a hundred different ways. I know that often to you, and always to the children, when I speak so, it sounds unendurably dull (it seems as though it were all well known); but I cannot help repeating that our happiness or unhappiness cannot in the least depend on whether we lose or acquire something, but only on what we ourselves are. [. . .] What our life together is, with our joys and sorrows, will appear to our children real life; and therefore it is important to help them to acquire what gave us happiness, and to help them to free themselves from what gave us unhappiness, but neither languages, nor diplomas, nor society, and still less, money, made our happiness or unhappiness. And therefore the question how much our income shrinks, cannot occupy me. If one attributes importance to that, it hides from us what really is important.

—Letter to Sofia Tolstaya, October 28, 1884

What, then, must we do? I have described my sufferings, my searchings, and my solution of this question, and I think the solution I have arrived at will be valid for all sincere men who set themselves the same question. First of all, to the question: What must we do? I replied to myself: I must not lie, either to myself or to others, nor fear the truth wherever it may lead me. [. . .] We consider lies to others [. . .] to be bad; but are not afraid of lying to ourselves; yet the very worst, most downright and deceptive lie to others is as nothing in its effects when compared with that lie to ourselves on which we have all built our lives.

—*What Then Must We Do?*

NIKOLAI IVANOVICH: . . . This may not be a convenient time, but heaven knows when we shall find a convenient time. Understand not me—but yourself: the meaning of your own life! We can't go on living like this without knowing what we are living for.

MARY IVANOVA: We have lived so, and lived very happily. [*Noticing a look of vexation on his face*] All right, all right, I am listening.

NIKOLAI IVANOVICH: Yes, I too lived so—that is to say, without thinking why I lived; but a time came when I was terror-struck. Well, here we are, living on other people's labor—making others work for us—bringing children into the world and bringing them up to do the same. Old age will come, and death, and I shall ask myself: "Why have I lived?" In order to breed more parasites like myself? And, above all, we do not even enjoy this life. It is only endurable, you know, while, like [our young son] Vanya, you overflow with life's energy.

—*The Light Shines in Darkness*

In reply to the question: What must I do? I saw that the most indubitable answer was, first, do all the things I myself need—attend to my own samovar, heat my own stove, fetch my water, attend to my clothes, and do all I can for myself. I thought this would seem strange to the servants; but it turned out that the strangeness only lasted for a week, and afterwards it would have seemed strange had I resumed my former habits.

To the question: Would it not absorb all my time and prevent my doing the mental work I love, to which I am accustomed, and which I sometimes consider useful? I received a most unexpected reply. The energy of my mental work increased, and increased in proportion to my bodily exertions.

—*What Then Must We Do?*

"What a delight it is to rest from intellectual occupations by means of simple physical labor! Every day, according to season, I either dig the ground, or saw and chop wood, or work with scythe, sickle, or some other instrument. As to plowing, you cannot conceive what a satisfaction it is to plow. It is not very hard work, as many people suppose; it is pure enjoyment! You go along, lifting up and properly directing the plow, and you don't notice how one, two, or three hours go by. The blood runs merrily through your veins; your head becomes clear; you don't feel the weight of your feet; and the appetite afterwards, and the sleep! . . . For me, daily exercise and physical labor are as indispensable as the air."

—*The Life of Tolstoy*,
conversation with Nikolay Danilevsky, 1886

The longer Levin mowed, the oftener he felt the moments of unconsciousness in which it seemed not his hands that swung the scythe, but the scythe mowing of itself, a body full of life and consciousness of its own, and as though by magic, without thinking of it, the work turned out regular and well-finished of itself. These were the most blissful moments.

—Anna Karenina

The moment you see an evil, even the smallest, try to mend it, to diminish it, and you will never see much evil at once and will not arrive at despair, and your hands will not drop, and you will do much good.

—Letter to D. R. Kudryavtsev, January 1887

The teaching of truth expressed by Christ is not contained in laws and commandments, but in one thing only—the meaning given to life. And that meaning is, that life and the blessing of life are not to be found in personal happiness, as people generally suppose, but in the service of God and man. And this is not a command which must be obeyed to gain a reward, nor is it a mystical expression of something mysterious and unintelligible, but it is the elucidation of a law of life previously concealed; it is the indication of the fact that life can be a blessing only when this truth is understood.

And, therefore, the whole positive teaching of Christ is expressed in this one thing: Love God and thy neighbor as thyself. And no expositions of that precept are possible. It is one, because it contains all. The law and commandments of Christ, like the Jewish and Buddhist laws and commandments, are but indications of cases in which the snares of the world turn men aside from a true understanding of life. And that is why there may be many laws and many commandments, but the positive teaching of life—of what should be done—must and can be only one.

—"Industry and Idleness"

What, then, must be done?

You know these things, and the teaching of truth tells you them. Go to the bottom—to what seems to you the bottom, but is really the top—take your place beside those who produce food for the hungry and clothes for the naked, and do not be afraid: it will not be worse, but better in all respects. Take your place in the ranks, set to work with your weak, unskilled hands at that primary work which feeds the hungry and clothes the naked: at bread-labor, the struggle with Nature; and you will feel, for the first time, firm ground beneath your feet, will feel that you are at home, that you are free and stand firmly, and have reached the end of your journey. And you will feel those complete, unpoisoned joys which can be found nowhere else—not secured by any doors nor screened by any curtains. You will know joys you have never known before; you will, for the first time, know those strong, plain men, your brothers, who from a distance have fed you until now; and to your surprise you will find in them such qualities as you have never known: such modesty, such kindness to yourself as you will feel you have not deserved.

—"Industry and Idleness"

[The painter K. P.] Bryullov one day corrected a pupil's study. The pupil, having glanced at the altered drawing, exclaimed: "Why, you only touched it a tiny bit, but it is quite another thing." Bryullov replied: "Art begins where the tiny bit begins."

That saying is strikingly true, not of art alone, but of all life. One may say that true life begins where the tiny bit begins—where what seem to us minute and infinitely small alterations take place. True life is not lived where great external changes take place—where people move about, clash, fight, and slay one another—but it is lived only where these tiny, tiny, infinitesimally small changes occur.

—"Why Do Men Stupefy Themselves?"

[. . .] man is a spiritual as well as an animal being. He may be moved by things that influence his spiritual nature, or by things that influence his animal nature, as a clock may be moved by its hands or by its main wheel. And just as it is best to regulate the movement of a clock by means of its inner mechanism, so a man—oneself or another—is best regulated by means of his consciousness. And as with a clock one has to take special care of that part by means of which one can best move the inner mechanism, so with a man one must take special care of the cleanness and clearness of consciousness which is the thing that best moves the whole man.

—"Why Do Men Stupefy Themselves?"

[. . .] the seeing, spiritual being, whose manifestation we commonly call conscience, always points with one end towards right and with the other towards wrong, and we do not notice it while we follow the course it shows: the course from wrong to right. But one need only do something contrary to the indication of conscience, to become aware of this spiritual being, which then shows how the animal activity has diverged from the direction indicated by conscience. And as a navigator, conscious that he is on the wrong track, cannot continue to work the oars, engine, or sails till he has adjusted his course to the indications of the compass, or has obliterated his consciousness of this divergence—each man who has felt the duality of his animal activity and his conscience can continue his activity only by adjusting that activity to the demands of conscience, or by hiding from himself the indications conscience gives him of the wrongness of his animal life.

—"Why Do Men Stupefy Themselves?"

"Faith—yes, we need faith. We can't do without faith. Not, however, faith in what other people tell us, but faith in what we arrive at ourselves, by our own thought, our own reason."

—*The Light Shines in Darkness*

"You see, if I say there is *a* God, the first cause of the Universe, everyone can agree with me; and such an acknowledgment of God will unite us; but if I say there is *the* God Brahma, or Jehovah, or a Trinity, such a God divides us. Men wish to unite, and to that end devise all means of union, but neglect the one indubitable means of union—the search for truth! It is as if people in an enormous building, where the light from above shone down into the center, tried to unite in groups around lamps in different corners, instead of going towards the central light, where they would naturally all be united."

—The Light Shines in Darkness

At the present moment I who am writing this and you who will read it, whoever you may be—have wholesome, sufficient, perhaps abundant and luxurious food, pure warm air to breathe, winter and summer clothing, various recreations, and, most important of all, leisure by day and undisturbed repose at night. And here by our side live the working people, who have neither wholesome food nor healthy lodgings nor sufficient clothing nor recreations, and who above all are deprived not only of leisure but even of rest: old men, children, women, worn out by labor, by sleepless nights, by disease, who spend their whole lives providing for us those articles of comfort and luxury which they do not possess, and which are for us not necessities but superfluities. Therefore a moral man (I do not say a Christian, but simply a man professing humane views or merely esteeming justice) cannot but wish to change his life and to cease to use articles of luxury produced under such conditions.

—"The First Step"

I much dislike, or rather am often uncomfortable, when people too well-disposed towards me take me seriously, seeking and demanding a complete correspondence between my words and my deeds. "How is it you say this, and do that?"

Yes, I am not a Saint, and have never given myself out for one. I am a man, often carried away; and sometimes, or rather always, saying not quite what I think and feel—not that I do not wish to say it, but that I am unable, and often exaggerate, or simply blunder. That is so in words. In deeds the case is yet worse. I am quite a weak man, of vicious habits, who wishes to serve the God of Truth, but constantly goes astray.

When people consider me as one who cannot make a mistake, every error seems like a lie or a piece of hypocrisy. But if I am understood to be a weak man, the discord between my words and acts appears as a sign of weakness, but not as a lie or a hypocrisy. And then I appear to be what I am: a sorry but sincere man, now and always wishing with his whole soul to be quite good; to be, that is, a worthy servant of God.

—Letter to D. A. Khilkov, February 1, 1892

. . . every man who has ever, even in childhood, experienced religious feeling, knows by personal experience that it was evoked in him, not by external, terrifying, material phenomena, but by an inner consciousness which had nothing to do with fear of the unknown forces of Nature—a consciousness of his own insignificance, loneliness, and guilt. And therefore, both by external observation and by personal experience, man may know that religion is not the worship of gods, evoked by superstitious fear of the invisible forces of Nature, proper to men only at a certain period of their development, but is something quite independent either of fear or of their degree of education—a something that cannot be destroyed by any development of culture. For man's consciousness of his finiteness amid an infinite universe, and of his sinfulness (i.e., of his not having done all he might and should have done) has always existed and will exist as long as man remains man.

—"Religion and Morality"

It is shameful to say how little is needed to set all men free from all the calamities which now oppress them; all that is needed is to give up lying. Only let men refuse to give in to the lie which is instilled into them, let them only not say what they do not think and what they do not feel, and at once there would be such a revolution in every stratum of our life as the revolutionists could not attain in centuries, even if all the power were in their hands.

If only men would believe that strength is not in force but in truth, and would boldly utter it, or at least would not depart from it in word and deed, would not say what they do not think, would not do what they consider wrong and stupid.

—"Christianity and Patriotism"

I had begun continuing on a fictional piece, but, if you can believe it, it was embarrassing to write about people who did not exist and did not do anything. Something wasn't right. Is this form of fiction obsolete, are stories obsolete, or am I obsolete?

—Letter to Nikolai Leskov, July 10, 1893

The highest artistic productions cannot be made on demand because the source of artistic work is the revelation of a new consciousness of life, which, by an ungraspable law, is created in the soul of the artist, and its expression shines on the path by which humankind may proceed.

—"On Art"

A writer is, after all, valuable to and needed by us only to the extent to which he opens to us the inner work of his soul. [. . .] the value to us in the writer's production is only that inner work of the soul, and not the architectural structure in which he in large part, I think, always mars them, and lays out his thoughts and feelings. Everything that Amiel put out in ready form—lessons, tracts, verses—was dead; his journal, where he wasn't thinking about the form, he was only talking to himself, is full of life, wisdom, consolation, and never stops being one of the best books that was accidentally given to us by people like Marcus Aurelius, Pascal, Epictetus.

—"Preface to Amiel's Journal"

Amiel's entire life as it is presented to us in his journal is full of this suffering, his wholehearted searching for God. And the contemplation of this search is all the more instructive in that it never stops being a search, never stands in one place, doesn't cross over to the consciousness of finding the truth or in didacticism. Amiel doesn't say to himself or to others: "I now know the truth—listen to me!" On the contrary, it seems to him, as it does to anyone who sincerely seeks the truth, that the more he finds out the more he needs to know, and he unceasingly does everything he can to more and more uncover the truth and therefore constantly feels himself ignorant.

—"Preface to Amiel's Journal"

Every man finds himself in his life in relation to truth in the position of a wanderer who walks in the dark by the light of a lantern moving in front of him: he does not see what is not yet illuminated by the lantern, nor what he has passed over and what is again enveloped in darkness, and it is not in his power to change his relation to either; but he sees, no matter on what part of the path he may stand, what is illuminated by the lantern, and it is always in his power to select one side of the road on which he is moving, or the other.

—*The Kingdom of God Is Within You*

Just as one jolt is sufficient for a liquid that is saturated with salt suddenly to become crystallized, thus, perhaps, the smallest effort will suffice for the truth, which is already revealed to men, to take hold of hundreds, thousands, millions of men,—for a public opinion to be established to correspond to the consciousness, and, in consequence of its establishment, for the whole structure of the existing life to be changed. And it depends on us to make this effort.

—*The Kingdom of God Is Within You*

Do not assert that you remain a landed proprietor, a manufacturer, a merchant, an artist, a writer, because this is useful for men; that you are serving as a governor, a prosecutor, a king, not because that gives you pleasure and you are used to it, but for the good of humanity; that you continue to be a soldier, not because you are afraid of punishment, but because you consider the army indispensable for the security of human life; you can always keep from lying thus to yourself and to men, and you are not only able, but even must do so, because in this alone, in the liberation of oneself from the lie and in the profession of the truth does the only good of your life consist.

You need but do this, and your position will inevitably change of its own accord.

—The Kingdom of God Is Within You

Try the experiment of ceasing to commit the cruel, treacherous, and base actions that you are constantly committing in order to retain your position, and you will lose it at once. Try the simple experiment, as a government official, of giving up lying, and refusing to take a part in executions and acts of violence; as a priest, of giving up deception; as a soldier, of giving up murder; as landowner or manufacturer, of giving up defending your property by fraud and force; and, you will at once lose the position which you pretend is forced upon you, and which seems burdensome to you.

A man cannot be placed against his will in a situation opposed to his conscience.

—The Kingdom of God Is Within You

"All these men, Maslennikov, and the inspector, and the convoy officer, if they were not governor, inspector, officer, would have considered twenty times before sending people in such heat in such a mass—would have stopped twenty times on the way, and, seeing that a man was growing weak, gasping for breath, would have led him into the shade, would have given him water and let him rest, and if an accident had still occurred they would have expressed pity. But they not only did not do it, but hindered others from doing it, because they considered not men and their duty towards them but only the office they themselves filled, and held what that office demanded of them to be above human relations.

"That's what it is," Nekhlyudov went on in his thoughts. "If one acknowledges but for a single hour that anything can be more important than love for one`s fellowmen, even in some one exceptional case, any crime can be committed without a feeling of guilt."

—*Resurrection*

To say a man should not be guided by reason is the same as to say to a man carrying a lamp in a dark catacomb that, to find the way out, he must extinguish his lamp and be guided, not by light, but by something else.

—"Reason and Religion"

". . . however great a gift for music you may have, and however much time and power you may spend on it, do remember that, above all, the most important of all is to be a man. It is always necessary to remember that art is not everything."

—In conversation with A. B. Goldenveiser, July 1896

A great teacher is great just because he is able to express the truth so that it can neither be hidden nor obscured, but is as plain as daylight. [. . .] The truth is there, for all who will read the Gospels with a sincere wish to know the truth, without prejudice and, above all without supposing that they contain some special sort of wisdom beyond human reason.

That is how I read the Gospels, and I found in them truth plain enough for little children to understand, as indeed is there said. [. . .] And therefore, to the question how Christ's teaching should be understood, I reply: "If you wish to understand it, read the Gospels, read them, putting aside all foregone conclusions; read them with the sole desire to understand what is there said. But just because the Gospels are holy books, read them considerately, reasonably, and with discernment, and not haphazard or mechanically, as though all the words were of equal weight."

—"How to Read the Gospels"

In my old age and state of health, I stand with one foot in the grave, and so human considerations have no meaning for me, and if they had some kind of meaning, I know that this presentation of my faith not only will not result in either my well-being or in people's kind opinion of me, but on the contrary it might only torment and aggravate unbelievers who demand literary writings from me, and not discussions about faith, so also the believers, who are tormented by all my religious writings and curse me for them. Besides which, by all probability, this writing will be unknown by people until after my death. Therefore I've convinced myself that I'm doing this not for the reward, nor for glory, nor worldly consideration, but only out of the fear of not fulfilling that which by me is wanted by whoever sent me to this earth, and to whom I every hour await my return.

And so I ask of all those who will read this to read and understand my writing, tossing aside that which, just as I did, all the worldly considerations, keeping in sight only the eternal source of truth and goodness, by the will of whom we came to this world and very soon as an existence will disappear from it, and without hurry and agitation, understand and judge that which I'm expressing; and in case of disagreement, without contempt or hatred but with pity and love correct me; and in case of agreement with me, to remember that if I speak the truth, that truth is not mine but God's, and that only by chance it proceeds through me, just as it proceeds through each of us when we recognize the truth and communicate it.

—"Preface to the Christian Teaching"

Because I am old, must I therefore not point out the evil which I clearly, unquestionably see, seeing it precisely because I am old and have lived and thought for long? Must a man who stands on the far side of the river, beyond the reach of that ruffian whom he sees compelling one man to murder another, not cry out to the slayer, bidding him to refrain, for the reason that such interference will still more enrage the ruffian? Moreover, I by no means see why the government, persecuting those who refuse military service, does not turn its punishment upon me, recognizing in me an instigator. I am not too old for persecution, for any and all sorts of punishments, and my position is a defenseless one. At all events, whether blamed and persecuted or not, whether those who refuse military service are persecuted or not, I, whilst I live, will not cease from saying what I now say; for I cannot refrain from acting according to my conscience.

—"The Beginning of the End"

". . . people think there are circumstances in which one may deal with human beings without love; and there are no such circumstances. One may deal with things without love. One may cut down trees, make bricks, hammer iron without love; but you cannot deal with people without it, just as one cannot deal with bees without being careful. If you deal carelessly with bees you will injure them, and will yourself be injured. And so with people. It cannot be otherwise, because natural love is the fundamental law of human life. It is true that a person cannot force another to love them, as he can force them to work for him; but it does not follow that a person may deal with people without love, especially to demand anything from them. If you feel no love, sit still," Nekhlyudov thought; "occupy yourself with things, with yourself, with anything you like, only not with people."

—*Resurrection*

Part 6

Approaching Death

Tolstoy suffered poor health, including malaria, in 1901–02 and spent ten months in Crimea recovering. His friend Vladimir Chertkov, while exiled by the Russian government and living in England, promoted and published his mentor's Christian and social justice writings. "Complete" editions of Tolstoy's works were published in English in 1899 and 1904. For several years, he wrote and revised his greatest novella, Hadji Murad, *about a brave and historical warrior from the Caucasus Mountains; he withheld its publication, however, possibly because of the exciting story's incongruity with his public advocacy of peace and nonviolence. Tolstoy's death in November 1910 was an international news event. He was indeed buried at the site at Yasnaya Polyana, where his oldest brother said the "green stick" was buried (see p. 6).*

". . . I write much, which is not good, because of an old man's ambition, a desire that all should think as I do."

—In conversation with Maxim Gorky [ca. 1901–02]

"All our actions are divided into those which have a value, and those which have no value at all, in the face of death. If I were told that I had to die tomorrow, I should not go out for a ride on horseback; but if I were about to die this moment, and Levochka here" (*Tolstoy's grandson, who passed across the terrace at that moment with his nurse*) "fell and burst into tears, I should run to him and pick him up. We are all in the position of passengers from a ship which has reached an island. We have gone on shore, we walk about and gather shells, but we must always remember that, when the whistle sounds, all the little shells will have to be thrown away and we must run to the boat."

—In conversation with A. B. Goldenveiser, July 7, 1900

I believe in this: I believe in God, whom I understand as Spirit, as Love, as the Source of all. I believe that he is in me and I in him. I believe that the will of God is most clearly and intelligibly expressed in the teaching of the man Jesus, whom to consider as God and pray to, I esteem the greatest blasphemy. I believe that man's true welfare lies in fulfilling God's will, and his will is that men should love one another and should consequently do to others as they wish others to do to them of which it is said in the Gospels that in this is the law. I believe therefore that the meaning of the life of every man is to be found only in increasing the love that is in him; that this increase of love leads man, even in this life, to ever greater and greater blessedness, and after death gives him the more blessedness the more love he has, and helps more than anything else towards the establishment of the Kingdom of God on earth: that is, to the establishment of an order of life in which the discord, deception, and violence that now rule will be replaced by free accord, by truth, and by the brotherly love of one for another.

—"Reply to the Synod's Edict"

Whether or not these beliefs of mine offend, grieve, or prove a stumbling-block to anyone, or hinder anything, or give displeasure to anybody, I can as little change them as I can change my body. I must myself live my own life and I must myself alone meet death (and that very soon), and therefore I cannot believe otherwise than as I—preparing to go to that God from whom I came—do believe. I do not believe my faith to be the one indubitable truth for all time, but I see no other that is plainer, clearer, or answers better to all the demands of my reason and my heart; should I find such a one I shall at once accept it, for God requires nothing but the truth.

—"Reply to the Synod's Edict"

I used to think it impossible to show people their mistake and sin without hurting them. "Is it possible to pull out a tooth without giving pain? Yes, cocaine and chloroform can allay physical suffering; but there is nothing of the kind for the soul." Thus I thought, but then immediately said to myself, "No; there *is* a spiritual chloroform. Here, as in other things, the body has been studied thoroughly, but the soul has not yet been considered. The operation of cutting off a leg or an arm is done with chloroform; whereas the operation of mending a man's soul is done without, and it hurts. That is why it often does not cure, but only causes a worse illness—that of ill-will. And yet there is a spiritual chloroform, and it is well known; it is always love."

—"The Root of the Evil"

I am now suffering the torments of hell: I am calling to mind all the infamies of my former life—these reminiscences do not pass away and they poison my existence. Generally people regret that the individuality does not retain memory after death. What a happiness that it does not! What an anguish it would be if I remembered in this life all the evil, all that is painful to the conscience, committed by me in a previous life. And, if one remembers the good, one has to remember the evil too. What a happiness that reminiscences disappear with death and that there only remains consciousness, a consciousness which, as it were, represents the general outcome of the good and the evil, like a complex equation reduced to its simplest expression: a positive or a negative, a great or a small quantity.

—"Reminiscences"

It is grievous to me, in my egotism, to have lived my life bestially, and to know that now it cannot be retrieved. Grievous, chiefly, because people will say: "It is all very well for you, a dying old man, to say this; but you did not live so! We too, when we are old, will say the same." That is where the chief punishment of sin lies; in feeling that one is an unworthy vessel for the transmission of the will of God— befouled and spoilt.

—*The Life of Tolstoy*

For three whole days, during which time did not exist for him, he struggled in that black sack into which he was being thrust by an invisible, resistless force. He struggled as a man condemned to death struggles in the hands of the executioner, knowing that he cannot save himself. And every moment he felt that despite all his efforts he was drawing nearer and nearer to what terrified him. He felt that his agony was due to his being thrust into that black hole and still more to his not being able to get right into it. He was hindered from getting into it by his conviction that his life had been a good one. That very justification of his life held him fast and prevented his moving forward, and it caused him the most torment of all.

—*The Death of Ivan Ilych*

Whether he admonished people, or simply blessed them, or prayed for the sick, or advised people about their lives, or listened to expressions of gratitude from those he had helped by precepts, or alms, or healing (as they assured him)—he could not help being pleased at it, and could not be indifferent to the results of his activity and to the influence he exerted. He thought himself a shining light, and the more he felt this the more was he conscious of a weakening, a dying down of the divine light of truth that shone within him. "In how far is what I do for God and in

84

how far is it for men?" That was the question that insistently tormented him and to which he was not so much unable to give himself an answer as unable to face the answer.

—*Father Sergius*

"Only one minute of life remains, and there's work for a hundred years."

—In conversation with A. B. Goldenveiser,
January 1905

"Immortality, incomplete, of course, is certainly realized in our children. How strongly man desires immortality is most clearly shown by his endeavor to leave some trace after his death. It might seem of no importance to a man what is said of him and whether he is remembered after he has gone; and yet what efforts he makes for it!"

—In conversation with A. B. Goldenveiser,
June 16, 1905

"In some old credulous woman you feel, in spite of the absurd superstition, that the foundation of her faith is a real striving for the highest and for the truth. Her outlook on the world is much higher than that of a professor who has solved all questions long ago."

—In conversation with A. B. Goldenveiser, July 6, 1905

"I used often to think that man cannot help having desires. I always had and still have desires [. . .] and all my wishes were either fulfilled and as soon as that happened ceased to attract me, or became impossible of fulfillment and I ceased to wish for them. But while my wishes were being fulfilled or becoming impossible, new wishes arose, and so it went on and goes on to the end. I wished for the winter—it has come; I wished for solitude—and have almost attained it; now I wish to describe my life, and to do it in the best way possible, that it may be of use to others. And whether this wish is fulfilled or not, new wishes will awaken. Life consists in that. And it occurs to me that if the whole of life consists in the birth of wishes and the joy of life lies in their fulfillment, then is there a wish which would be natural to man, to every human being, always, and would always be fulfilled or rather would be approaching fulfillment? And it has become clear to me that this would be so for a man who desired death. His whole life would be an approach to the fulfillment of that wish and the wish would certainly be fulfilled."

—"Fedor Kuzmich"

"It is surprising how all the past becomes me. It is in me, like something folded. But it is difficult to be perfectly sincere. Sometimes I remember the bad only, another time the opposite. Lately I have remembered only the bad acts and events. It is difficult in this to keep the balance, so as not to exaggerate one way or another."

—In conversation with A. B. Goldenveiser,
August 1, 1905

"In old age one becomes indifferent to the fact that one will never see the results of one's activity. But the results will be there."

—In conversation with A. B. Goldenveiser,
January 6, 1908

"In the past, I remember, I experienced a feeling of pride; I was glad at my success. But now—and I think it is not false modesty—it is a matter of absolute indifference to me. Perhaps it is because I have had too much success. It is like sweets: if you have too many, you feel surfeited. But one thing is pleasant: in nearly all the letters, congratulations, addresses, the same thing is repeated—it has simply become a truism—that I have destroyed religious delusions and opened the way for the search after truth. If it is true, it is just what I have wanted and tried to do all my life, and this is very dear to me."

—In conversation with A. B. Goldenveiser after having
received two thousand telegrams of congratulation
on his eightieth birthday, August 28, 1908

You seem to think that you and those who taught you are the only people who know the truth, and that all the rest are lost. I do not think I am the only person who knows the truth and that everyone else is in darkness. I am eighty years old, and I am still searching for truth. Your teachers have misled you into the sin of pride and condemnation. Every man in the depths of his soul has something he alone comprehends, namely his attitude toward God. And this sphere is sacred. We must not attempt to invade it or to imagine that we know all that lies hidden in its depths.

—Letter to an Old Believer, December 16, 1908

I cannot but feel that there is an indubitable interdependence between my spacious room, my dinner, my clothing, my leisure, and the terrible crimes committed to get rid of those who would like to take from me what I have. And though I know that these homeless, embittered, depraved people— who but for the government's threats would deprive me of all I am using—are products of that same government's actions, still I cannot help feeling that at present my peace really is dependent on all the horrors that are now being perpetrated by the government. And being conscious of this I can no longer endure it, but must free myself from this intolerable position!

It is impossible to live so! I, at any rate, cannot and will not live so. That is why I write this and will circulate it by all means in my power both in Russia and abroad—that one of two things may happen: either that these inhuman deeds may be stopped, or that my connection with them may be snapped and I put in prison, where I may be clearly conscious that these horrors are not committed on my behalf; or still better (so good that I dare not even dream of such happiness) that they may put on me, as on those twelve or twenty peasants, a shroud and a cap and may push me also off a bench, so that by my own weight I may tighten the well-soaped noose round my old throat.

—"I Cannot Be Silent"

Before us are millions of armed men, ever more and more efficiently armed and trained for more and more rapid slaughter. We know that these millions of people have no wish to kill their fellows and for the most part do not even know why they are forced to do that repulsive work, and that they are weary of their position of subjection and compulsion; we know that the murders committed from time to time by these men are committed by order of the governments; and we know that the existence of the governments depends on the armies. [. . .]

But how will nations defend themselves against their enemies, how will they maintain internal order, and how can nations live without an army? What form of life men will take after they repudiate murder we do not and cannot know; but one thing is certain: that it is more natural for men to be guided by reason and conscience with which they are endowed than to submit slavishly to people who arrange wholesale murders; and that therefrom the form of social order assumed by the lives of those who are guided in their actions not by violence based on threats of murder, but by reason and conscience, will in any case be no worse than that under which they now live.

That is all I want to say. I shall be sorry if it offends or grieves anyone or evokes any ill feeling. But for me, a man eighty years old, expecting to die at any moment, it would be shameful and criminal not to speak out the whole truth as I understand it—the truth which, as I firmly believe, is alone capable of relieving mankind from the incalculable ills produced by war.

—Address to the Swedish Peace Congress
("Last Message to Mankind"), August 1909

The longer I live—especially now when I clearly feel the approach of death—the more I feel moved to express what I feel more strongly than anything else, and what in my opinion is of immense importance, namely, what we call the renunciation of all opposition by force, which really simply means the doctrine of the law of love unperverted by sophistries. Love, or in other words the striving of men's souls towards unity and the submissive behavior to one another that results therefrom, represents the highest and indeed the only law of life, as every man knows and feels in the depths of his heart . . .

—Letter to M. K. Gandhi, September 7, 1910

Another bullet hit Hadji Murad in the left side. He lay down in the ditch and again pulled some cotton wool out of his beshmet and plugged the wound. This wound in the side was fatal and he felt that he was dying. Memories and pictures succeeded one another with extraordinary rapidity in his imagination. Now he saw the powerful Abu Nutsal Khan, dagger in hand and holding up his severed cheek as he rushed at his foe; then he saw the weak, bloodless old Vorontsov with his cunning white face, and heard his soft voice; then he saw his son Yusuf, his wife Sofiat, and then the pale, red-bearded face of his enemy Shamil with its half-closed eyes. All these images passed through his mind without evoking any feeling within him—neither pity nor anger nor any kind of desire: everything seemed so insignificant in comparison with what was beginning, or had already begun, within him. [. . .] When Hadji Aga, who was the first to reach him, struck him on the head with a large dagger, it seemed to Hadji Murad that someone was striking him with a hammer and he could not understand who was doing it or why. That was his last consciousness of any connection with his body. He felt nothing more and his enemies kicked and hacked at what had no longer anything in common with him.

—Hadji Murad

The question how the world had originated did not interest him, just because the question how it would be best to live in this world was ever before him. He never thought about future life, always bearing in the depth of his soul the firm and quiet conviction inherited from his forefathers, and common to all laborers on the land, that just as in the world of plants and animals nothing ceases to exist, but continually changes its form, the manure into grain, the grain into a food, the tadpole into a frog, the caterpillar into a butterfly, the acorn into an oak, so man also does not perish, but only undergoes a change. He believed in this, and therefore always looked death straight in the face, and bravely bore the sufferings that lead towards it, but did not care and did not know how to speak about it.

—Resurrection

. . . he died only this year—at home and under the ikons, with a lighted wax candle in his hands, just as he had always wished. Before his death he took leave of his old wife, and pardoned her for the cooper. He took leave also of his son and grandchildren, and died thoroughly happy to think that his death left his son and daughter-in-law freed from the burden of having a supernumerary mouth to feed, and that this time he himself would really pass from a life which had grown wearisome to him to that other life which had been growing more and more familiar and alluring to him each year and hour. Is he better or worse off now where he has awakened after his death—the death which really came that time? Is he disillusioned, or has he really found what he expected? Soon we shall all know.

—*Master and Man*

Selected Bibliography and List of Translators

Tolstoy's Works

Dole, Nathan Haskell. (Trans.). *The Complete Works of Lyof N. Tolstoi*. New York: E. R. DuMont, 1899.

Maude, Aylmer & Maude, Louise. (Trans.). *The Works, Centenary Edition*. 21 volumes. Oxford: Oxford University Press, 1928–38.

Polnoe Sobranie Sochinenii (Complete Collected Works). 90 volumes. Moscow: Khudozhestvennaia Literatura, 1928–58.

Wiener, Leo. (Trans.). *The Complete Works of Count Tolstoy*. 24 volumes. Boston: D. Estes, 1904.

Biographies, Studies, Collections, and Memoirs Cited or Consulted

Bartlett, Rosamund. *Tolstoy: A Russian Life*. London: Profile Books, 2010.

Bayley, John. (Ed.). *The Portable Tolstoy*. New York: Penguin, 1978.

Birukoff, Paul. [Pavel Biryukov.] *Leo Tolstoy: His Life and Work and Biographical Material, Compiled by Paul Birukoff, and Revised by Leo Tolstoy: Childhood and Early Manhood*. New York: Charles Scribner's Sons, 1911.

Blaisdell, Bob. *Creating Anna Karenina: Tolstoy and the Birth of Literature's Most Enigmatic Heroine*. New York: Pegasus, 2020.

Burnasheva, N. I. (Ed.). *L. N. Tolstoy Entsiklopediya* [Encyclopedia]. Moscow: Prosveshchenie, 2009.

Christian, R. F. (Ed.). *Tolstoy's Letters*. New York: Charles Scribner's Sons, 1978.

Christian, R. F. (Ed., Trans.). *Tolstoy's Diaries*. New York: The Scribner Press, 1985.

Goldenweizer, A. B. [Goldenveiser]. *Talks with Tolstoy*. Translated by S. S. Koteliansky and Virginia Woolf. London: The Hogarth Press, 1923.

Gorky, Maxim. *Reminiscences of Leo Nikolaevich Tolstoy*. Translated by S. S. Koteliansky and Leonard Woolf. New York: B. W. Huebsch, 1920.

Gusev, N. N. *Lev Nikolaevich Tolstoy: Materials for a Biography from 1870 to 1881*. Moscow: Akademii Nauk, 1963.

Maude, Aylmer. *The Life of Tolstoy, First Fifty Years*. 2nd ed. London: A. Constable and Company, Ltd, 1908.

Maude, Aylmer. *The Life of Tolstoy, Later Years*. London: A. Constable and Company, Ltd, 1910.

Polner, Tikhon. *Tolstoy and His Wife*. New York: Norton, 1945.

Simmons, Ernest J. *Leo Tolstoy*. New York: Vintage, 1960.

Tolstoy, Alexandra [Tolstaya]. *Tolstoy: A Life of My Father*. New York: Harper and Brothers, 1953.

Tolstoy, Leo. *Selected Essays*. New York: The Modern Library, 1964.

Tolstoy, Leo. *Writings on Civil Disobedience and Non-Violence*. New York: Signet, 1968.

Tolstoy, Leo. *Lev Tolstoy: Short Stories*. Moscow: Progress Publishers, 1975.

Tolstoy, Leo. *A Calendar of Wisdom*. Translated by Peter Sekirin. New York: Scribner, 1997.

Tolstoy, Leo. *Lives and Deaths: Essential Stories*. Translated by Boris Dralyuk. London: Pushkin Press, 2019.

Tolstoy, Leo. *On Life: A Critical Edition*. Translated by Michael A. Denner and Inessa Medzhibovskaya. Evanston, IL: Northwestern University Press, 2019.

Zorin, Andrei. *Leo Tolstoy*. London: Reaktion Books, 2020.

Quoted Works and Their Dates of Composition and/or Publication (Translators' Initials are Listed in Brackets)

Address to the Swedish Peace Congress, essay (1909) [AM]

Anna Karenina, novel, 1873–77 (1878) [CG]

"The Beginning of the End," essay (1896) [NHD]

Boyhood, novella, 1852–54 (1854) [BB]

Childhood, novella, 1851–52 (1852) [BB]

"Christianity and Patriotism," essay (1894) [CG]

"Church and State," essay, 1879–86 (1886) [NHD]

The Cossacks, novel, 1852–62 (1863) [AM]

Diary entries: March 17, 1847 [BB]; April 17, 1847 [BB]; June 29, 1852 [PB]; July 3, 1854 [AM]; July 7, 1854 [AM]; March 5, 1855 [PB]; September 17, 1855 [BB]

Family Happiness, novella, 1858–59 (1859) [AM]

Father Sergius, novella, 1890–1900 (1911) [AM]

"Fedor Kuzmich," unfinished story, 1905–07 (1912) [AM]

"First Recollections," memoirs, 1878 (1906) [PB]

"The First Step," essay, 1891–92 (1892) [AM]

Hadji Murad, novella, 1896–1904 (1912) [AM]

"How to Read the Gospels," essay (1896) [AM]

"I Cannot Be Silent," essay (1908) [AM]

"Industry and Idleness," essay (1888) [AM]

"Introduction to an Examination of the Gospels," essay (1880) [AM]

The Kingdom of God Is Within You, religious work, 1890–93 (1893) [LW[1]]

"A Landed Proprietor," story (1856) [LW]

Letters: February 13, 1849 [PB]; January 12, 1852 [PB]; December 1874 [BB]; January 1883 [AM]; July 1884 [AM]; January 1887 [LW]; February 1, 1892 [AM]; July 10, 1893 [BB]; December 16, 1908 [AM]; September 7, 1910 [AM]

The Life of Tolstoy by Aylmer Maude, biography (1908–10) [AM]

*The Light Shines in Darkne*ss, play, ca. 1890 (1912) [LAM]

Master and Man, novella, 1894–95 (1895) [NHD]

"Notes of a Madman," unfinished story, mid-1880s (1912) [CG]

"On Art," ca. 1895–97 (1929) [BB]

"On Popular Education," essay (1862) [BB]

"Preface to Amiel's Journal," essay (1893) [BB]

"Preface to the Christian Teaching," essay (1891) [BB]

---

[1] Wiener translates all but the final quoted passage from *The Kingdom of God Is Within You* ("Try this experiment . . ." is translated by Constance Garnett).

"Reason and Religion," essay, mid-1890s (1897) [AM]

"Religion and Morality," essay (1893) [AM]

"Reminiscences," memoirs, 1901–03 (1903) [PB]

Reminiscences of Leo Nikolaevich Tolstoy by Maxim Gorky, memoir (1920) [KW]

"Reply to the Synod's Edict," essay (1901) [AM]

Resurrection, novel, 1895–99 (1899) [LM]

Talks with Tolstoy by A. B. Goldenveiser [Gol'denveiser], memoir (1921) [KVW]

"The Root of the Evil," essay, (1901) [AM]

War and Peace, novel, 1863–69 (1869) [CG]

What I Believe, religious work, 1883–84 (1884) [NHD]

What Then Must We Do?, religious work, 1882–86 (1902) [AM]

"Why Do Men Stupefy Themselves?" essay (1891) [AM]

Youth, novella, 1855–57 (1857) [BB]

Translators

Pavel Birukov[2] [PB]

Bob Blaisdell [BB]

Nathan Haskell Dole [NHD]

Constance Garnett [CG]

S. S. Kotliansky and Leonard Woolf [KW]

---

[2] The passages I attribute here to Birukov were almost certainly not translated by Birukov himself, as the passages from Tolstoy's fiction that he quotes in the biography are identical to those of Leo Wiener's 1904 translations in *The Complete Works of Count Tolstoy*. No translator is credited in any of Birukov's English editions.

S. S. Kotliansky and Virginia Woolf [KVW]

Aylmer Maude [AM]

Louise Maude [LM]

Aylmer *and* Louise Maude [LAM]

Leo Wiener [LW]